Common Sense

A Second American Revolution

Les Livingstone

1

Dedication

To Trudy, with love.

Table of Contents

Chapter 1

Introduction

America is a land of taxation that was founded to avoid taxation.
Laurence J. Peter

"Common Sense" is the book published by Thomas Paine in January 1776. It was an instant bestseller, not only in America but also in the other British colonies and in Europe. This brilliant political pamphlet was a significant part of the inspiration for the American Revolution. Common Sense advocated an immediate declaration of independence from Britain, because Britain imposed taxation and other demands on America, but denied representation to the American colonies. This gave rise to the revolutionary cry of taxation without representation!

Thomas Paine was born in England and worked as an excise officer. He was dismissed from his post when lobbying for higher wages. Paine had favorably impressed Benjamin Franklin, who sponsored Paine's immigration to America in 1774. In Philadelphia Paine became a journalist and contributed articles to The Pennsylvania Magazine.

The major points of Common Sense can be summarized as follows:

<u>Major Points of Common Sense</u>:
1. Government is society's sacrifice of liberty in exchange for security.
2. The British government imposes taxation, but withholds representation of the American colonies.
3. The British government is remote and distant, but American needs are pressing and local.
4. The interests of government and the governed are very different

Paine's Common Sense challenged the authority of the British Crown in plain straightforward language that spoke powerfully to the common people of America. It went far in energizing the American Revolution. But all of this is old history, dating back to the distant past in 1776. What does it matter now, more than 230 years after 1776? Isn't it only of academic and historical interest, but irrelevant to our concerns in the 21st century?

Some things never change, but remain of enduring significance. In 2010 Congress passed Obamacare despite the opposition of a majority of U.S. voters. Also, the government "stimulus" designed by our government to combat unemployment has dismally failed to reduce unemployment and is opposed by a majority of U.S. voters. Congress and the U.S. president have spent massive funds, far beyond all available tax monies paid by taxpayers and have borrowed enormous sums by issuing treasury securities. In addition to these debt obligations, the government has gigantic unfunded liabilities for future payments under Social Security, Medicare, and Medicaid. These liabilities will inflict vast obligations upon our children and grandchildren and their descendants. In turn, massive tax increases are likely to be imposed in order to pay off these obligations. In short, we are exactly in the same position today as the founders of America were in 1776. Taxation without representation is a pressing problem today, just as it was in 1776.

U.S. Government Debt,

Just how much is U.S. government debt, and how has it changed over a number of years? The relevant figures are shown below in Table 1-1. Total Public Debt Outstanding represents all U.S. federal government borrowing through treasury securities. By way of comparison, we include a column for U.S. GDP. GDP is gross domestic product, which is the value of all goods and services produced by labor and property located in the United States. In order to provide a measure of government borrowing Table 1-1 shows the conventional yardstick of Total Public Debt Outstanding as a percentage of GDP.

Year	Total Public Debt Outstanding ($billion)[1]	Gross Domestic Product ($billion)[2]	% Public Debt to GDP
1998	$5,565	$8,793.5	63%
1999	$5,672	$9,353.5	61%
2000	$5,678	$9,951.5	57%
2001	$5,770	$10,286.2	56%

---

[1] As of August 31 each year
http://www.treasurydirect.gov/NP/BPDLogin?application=np
[2] http://www.bea.gov/national/#gdp Year 2010 is estimated.

2002	$6,210	$10,642.3	58%
2003	$6,790	$11,142.1	61%
2004	$7,351	$11,867.8	62%
2005	$7,927	$12,638.4	63%
2006	$8,515	$13,398.9	64%
2007	$9,006	$14,061.8	64%
2008	$9,646	$14,369.1	67%
2009	$11,813	$14,119.3	84%
2010	$13,450	$14,359.3	94%

Table 1-1

From Table 1-1 we see that in the nine years from 1998 to 2007 the Total Public Debt Outstanding hovered between 56% and 64% of GDP. But since 2007 Total Public Debt Outstanding has jumped up all the way to 94% of GDP in 2010. In fact, from 2007 (when the Democrats gained the majority in Congress) to 2010 the average annual increase in Total Public Debt Outstanding was 14.3%, which is more than 3 times the average annual rate of growth of 4.75% from 1998-2004. During the same years 2007 to 2010, GDP grew at an average annual rate of only 2.3%. So from 2007-2010 Total Public Debt Outstanding grew at an average annual rate of 14.3% while GDP grew at only a 2.3% average annual rate. That is a very significant difference. Clearly the U.S. government was piling on debt a great deal faster than the U.S. economy was growing. It should be pointed out that both Democrat and Republican politicians are complicit in greatly over-spending federal, state and local government budgets. While the Democrats have the worse record, the Republicans are far from blameless. So this is not a partisan debate – it is

7

profoundly distrustful of both parties and of most politicians.

Unfunded Government Liabilities

Another way to look at our current Total Public Debt Outstanding of $13,450 billion is to divide it by our current population of 300 million people. This amounts to $44,833 for every man, woman and child in America. As significant as our per capita Total Public Debt Outstanding may be, it pales in comparison to our total unfunded liabilities for unfunded promises made by federal, state and local governments. From USA Today these liabilities are as shown in Table 1-2 below:[3]:

The cost per U.S. household of unfunded promises made by federal, state and local government:

Medicare	$255,280
Social Security	$144,251
Federal Debt	$43,380
Military Benefits	$25,863
State and local debt	$17,537
Federal civil-servant benefits	$14,374
State and local retiree benefits	$13,114
Other federal obligations	$2,548
Total	$516,348

Table 1-2

---

[3] http://www.usatoday.com/news/washington/2007-05-28-federal-budget_N.htm

As Table 1-2 shows, the average cost per U.S. household of unfunded promises made by federal, state and local government is the huge amount of $516,348. How will federal, state, and local governments pay these liabilities? Since federal, state, and local governments have not funded these obligations, they have to collect enough money from citizens to pay for their commitments. These liabilities can only be paid out of taxes[4]. This raises the question of whether U.S. households can afford to pay taxes averaging $516,348 per household. In other words, does the average U.S. household have sufficient means to shoulder a debt burden of $516,348?

The amount of $516,348 is way beyond the 2008 U.S. Census Bureau median household income of $52,029[5]. It is also way beyond the $120,300 U.S. Census Bureau 2007 median household net worth[6]. Therefore it is extremely difficult to see how U.S. households can afford to pay this cost of $516,348 per household when the median household income is only $52,029, and median household net worth is only $120,300. Ask yourself if you would make an unsecured loan of $516,348 to a family with annual income of $52,029 and net worth of $120,300? The only sensible answer is certainly not!

---

[4] The government can defer payment by borrowing. But eventually this borrowing must be paid off by tax collections, and interest has to be paid on the borrowing. So, in the last analysis, all government debt must be paid out of tax collections.

[5] http://quickfacts.census.gov/qfd/states/00000.html

[6] Net worth is the excess of what is owned over what is owed. For example, if one owns $100 and owes $20, then one's net worth is $100 - $20 = $80.

Before World War II U.S. Public debt tended to be well below 40% of gross domestic product (GDP)[7].

Look at it this way. With annual income of $52,029 a household would do well to save 10% a year, which is $5,200[8]. So the household net worth could grow by $5,200 each year. With a current net worth of $120,300 next year's net worth would be $120,300 + $5,200 = $125,500. The following year's net worth would be $125,500 + $5,200 = $130,700. When would household net worth reach the $516,348 required to pay off the average debt burden per household? From the debt burden of $516,348 we subtract the current net worth of $120,300 per household, which leaves $396,048. At $5,200 per year, it would take a little more than 76 years to reach $516,348.

Once the debt burden of $516,348 has been paid off, the average household will owe no more, but will have a zero net worth. So our calculation reveals that it would reasonably take 76 years for the average U.S. household just to get out of debt with zero net worth. And 76 years is equivalent to about 3 generations.[9] In other words, our federal, state, and local governments have already overspent our resources for the next 76 years or 3 generations.

---

[7] Source:
http://www.usgovernmentspending.com/federal_debt_chart.html

[8] This is a very generous assumption: it implicitly takes for granted that the average breadwinners will not lose their jobs, fall ill or become disabled. It also assumes a high savings rate of 10% of income.

[9] A generation is generally considered to be about 25 years, which is the average number of years from the birth of a parent to the birth of a child.

We are in hock up to our eyeballs – in fact we are in hock up to our grandchildren's' eyeballs. We are deeply in debt for the next 3 generations to come. Our politicians have been on a spending spree that makes drunken sailors seem sober and prudent![10]!

Taxation Without Representation

It is time to summarize our discussion so far. The majority of U.S. citizens are against the government's imposition of Obama-care. The majority of U.S. citizens are also against the government's imposition of a massive "stimulus" that has failed miserably to produce the promised new jobs in order to overcome our current unemployment. The Gallup Poll estimates both the percentage unemployed and the percentage of those working part-time but wanting full-time work. It is based on more than 17,000 phone interviews with U.S. adults aged 18 and older in the workforce, is collected over a 30-day period. In mid-2010 this rate stood at 19.1%.[11] The 19.1% consists of 9.7% unemployment plus an additional 9.4% underemployment. Clearly a rate as high as 19.1% is extremely serious and shows that our economy is in a very serious downturn that is causing great distress to many American families.

There is widespread dissatisfaction with government policies that have failed to provide relief from economic hardship. At the same time,

---

[10] In all fairness to drunken sailors, they are reckless with their own money – unlike politicians who waste the taxpayers' money with reckless abandon.

[11] http://www.gallup.com/poll/139346/no-improvement-gallup-underemployment-rate-may.aspx

enormous government expenditures have created an average cost per U.S. household of unfunded promises in the huge amount of $516,348. This huge sum will sooner or later result in massive tax increases accompanied by wholesale reductions in social security, Medicare and Medicaid benefits. This pattern represents taxation without representation, just as it did in 1776. We have come full circle from 1776, and once more we face taxation without representation. It is time for a second American revolution. The only difference is that the first American Revolution was against the British crown. The second American Revolution is not against the British crown, but against an American government that has become just as oppressive and just as callous as the British crown.

U.S. public debt was below 40% of GDP from 1792 until World War II. After World War II the U.S. public debt fell below 40% of GDP again through the early 1980's. Clearly the USA proved that it could be the most prosperous nation in the world with a public debt below 40% of GDP. However, after the early 1980's the U.S. public debt rose higher and higher in most years as a percentage of GDP. By 2010 it was almost back to its peak during World War II, despite the fact that no world war was being fought in the 21st century. Currently, U.S. public debt is almost 100% of GDP. How does this compare with other countries? Using 2009 figures, only 10 of 129 countries had public debt amounting to more than 100% of GDP [12]. And these 10 countries included basket cases such as Zimbabwe,

---

[12] Source: https://www.cia.gov/library/publications/the-world-factbook/rankorder/2186rank.html

Greece, Italy, Iceland, Sudan, Lebanon and Jamaica. Clearly the USA at nearly 100% of GDP is entering dangerous territory.

The federal government collects taxes in order to finance various public services. It is informative to examine what the government does with the money it collects. In fiscal year 2010, the federal government is projected to spend $3.6 trillion. This amounts to 24% of GDP. The major items in the budget largely resemble the pattern of recent years. Of that $3.6 trillion, almost $2.2 trillion will be financed by federal tax revenues. The remaining $1.4 trillion will be financed by borrowing; This $1.4 trillion deficit will ultimately be paid for by future taxpayers. As shown in the table below, three major areas of spending each individually make up about one-fifth of the budget, and collectively add up to 55%[13]:

- **Social Security:** In 2010 about 20% of the budget will pay for Social Security, which provided retirement benefits averaging $1,117 per month to 36 million retired workers (and their eligible dependents) in December 2009. Social Security also provided survivors' benefits to 6.4 million surviving children and spouses of deceased workers and disability benefits to 9.7 million disabled workers and their eligible dependents in December 2009.
- **Medicare, Medicaid, and CHIP:** Three health insurance programs — Medicare, Medicaid, and the Children's Health

---

[13] Source: http://www.cbpp.org/cms/?fa=view&id=1258

Insurance Program (CHIP) together account for 21% of the budget in 2010. Nearly two-thirds of this amount goes to Medicare, which provides health coverage to around 46 million people who are over the age of 65 or have disabilities. The remainder of this category funds Medicaid and CHIP, which in 2010 will provide health care or long-term care to about 64 million low-income children, parents, elderly people, and people with disabilities. Medicaid and CHIP both require matching payments from the states.

- **Safety net programs:** About 14% of the 2010 federal budget supports programs that provide aid (other than health insurance or Social Security benefits) to individuals and families facing hardship. These programs include the refundable portion of the earned-income and child tax credits, (which assist low- and moderate-income working families through the tax code); programs that provide cash payments to eligible individuals or households, including Supplemental Security Income for the elderly or disabled poor and unemployment insurance; various forms of in-kind assistance for low-income families and individuals, including food stamps, school meals, low-income housing assistance, child-care assistance, and assistance in meeting home energy bills; and various other programs such as those that aid abused and neglected children.

We need to explore this territory in some detail. The federal government budget consists of the following major categories in Table 1-3 below:

Defense & Security	20%
Safety Net Programs	**14%**
Medicare, Medicaid &	
CHIP	**21%**
Social Security	**20%**
Other	25%
Total	100%

Table 1-3

The three categories in bold type in Table 1-3 above are income transfers from those paying in to those receiving the benefits. They add up to a combined 55% of the federal government budget. In other words, the single greatest category of federal government expenditures consists of these entitlements to benefits. How can government meet its obligations to pay these promised entitlement benefits to the recipients? The reality seems to be that government will not keep its promise to provide these entitlement benefits. Here is why.

Due to the reckless negligence of our politicians we are faced with an insurmountable mountain of unfunded liabilities. In order to pay these liabilities taxation would need to be raised to unsustainable levels, and government expenditures would need to be slashed by huge amounts. But politicians have proved to be unwilling to risk their seats by raising taxes to unsustainable levels. Politicians have also repeatedly shown a complete disregard for cutting government expenditures.

In fact, throughout the history of the U.S. budget deficits rather than budget surpluses have been routine.

Clearly our politicians are addicted to deficit spending, and are unaccustomed to the fiscal discipline of living within one's means. In that case, what can we reasonably expect to happen with the huge overhang of unfunded government liabilities, payment of which will require massive future tax increases? There seem to be only two alternatives, as follows:

1. Government will probably renege on its promised entitlement benefits. For example, the ages of eligibility for Medicare and Social Security will probably be raised, and the benefits will probably be strictly rationed by disallowing or delaying surgical operations such as organ transplants of hearts, kidneys and other vital body parts, knee or hip replacements, and other costly medical procedures.

2. Government will be tempted to print money with abandon – which would lead to inflation[14]. Inflation reduces the purchasing power of money. That benefits debtors like the federal government by reducing the burden of repaying the mammoth federal debt. They will repay the big dollars they borrowed with little dollars of lower

---

[14] Inflation results from more money chasing the same supply of goods. As a result prices soar higher – in other words, the dollar loses value because the same number of dollars can purchase fewer goods.

16

purchasing power. This is a very tempting policy for the federal government, because printing money and causing inflation is like a tax. It benefits the government, while at the same time it reduces the resources of taxpayers. Taxpayer disposable incomes fall in purchasing power, and taxpayer savings lose value.

In these circumstances it appears highly likely that government will slash Medicare and Social Security benefits, and will be sorely tempted to print money with wild abandon. This raises a number of questions. For example:

1. Is there an optimal size of government for economic prosperity and growth?
2. If so, what size should government be in relation to the total economy?
3. Which functions in the economy are best performed by the government, and which functions should not be performed by government?
4. How should government functions be divided among federal, state, and local governments?
5. What fact-based evidence and logical arguments exist in order for us to best decide these important issues?

The purpose of this book is to try and answer these questions. In seeking answers to these questions we need to revisit some familiar territory, such as capitalism versus socialism, communism, and fascism. We will not simply re-plough some old furrows. Rather we will try to be concise, practical, and decisive. We begin with Chapter 2, which discusses whether government or the private sector should be responsible for allocating scarce economic resources to the infinite demands of producers and consumers.

Chapter Summary

The main points of Chapter 1 are as follows:

1. Thomas Paine's book "Common Sense" was a significant part of the inspiration for the 1776 American Revolution. It protested against taxation by the British crown without representation in the British parliament.
2. Today we seem to have come full circle in being under an unresponsive federal government of reckless spenders who have dug our nation into a vast fiscal hole that foreshadow unsustainable future taxes that neither our children nor our grandchildren can afford to pay.
3. Rather than acting responsibly to cut federal expenditures, our irresponsible politicians are likely to ration healthcare by denying costly but necessary medical procedures, and by launching inflation by rashly printing excessive amounts of money.
4. This raises a number of questions, such as:
   a. Is there an optimal size of government for economic prosperity and growth?
   b. If so, what size should government be in relation to the total economy?

   c. Which functions in the economy are best performed by the government, and which functions should not be performed by government?

   d. How should government functions be divided among federal, state, and local governments?

   e. What fact-based evidence and logical arguments exist in order for us to best decide these important issues?

The purpose of this book is to try and answer these questions. We begin with Chapter 2, which discusses whether government or the private sector should be responsible for allocating scarce economic resources to the infinite demands of producers and consumers.

Chapter 2

What Government Should and Should Not Do

Government big enough to supply everything you need is big enough to take everything you have. The course of history shows us that as a government grows, liberty decreases. *Thomas Jefferson*

Scarcity exists everywhere, because human desires always exceed the available supply. Demand for resources tends to be greater than what can be provided. Scarcity guarantees that people will compete for resources Markets are one way to organize and channel this competition for resources. Politics is another way to allocate resources. People use both markets and politics in order to get resources allocated to the uses they favor. Even in a democracy, however, political activity is startlingly different from voluntary exchange in markets.

The theoretical extremes are total free markets at one end of the scale, and complete totalitarianism at the opposite end. We use the term "totalitarian" to include socialist, communist, and fascist regimes because all of these regimes are characterized by a large, powerful government that tolerates no open dissent and allows little, if any, individual liberty or free expression. In practice there are few, if any, economies that are purely free enterprise or – at the opposite pole – purely totalitarian. Even in Soviet Russia under Joseph Stalin there was a black market. In many totalitarian regimes there are large underground markets. In extreme cases the underground economy is as big as, or even bigger than, the official economy. At the opposite extreme, even the most free enterprise economies have some government functions.

In practice, virtually all economies are mixed, with some activities carried out by the government, and other activities carried out in the private sector. So the issue of government sector and private sector becomes which economic activities should be performed by government, and which economic activities should be performed in the private sector? At the totalitarian extreme, the bulk of economic activity is in the government sector. Examples are Cuba, North Korea, Iran, Zimbabwe and Libya. At the free enterprise extreme the bulk of economic activity is in the private sector. Examples are Hong Kong, Singapore, Australia, New Zealand and Switzerland[15].

The countries that enjoy the most economic freedom from government intervention are the most economically prosperous. The countries that enjoy the least economic freedom from government intervention are the least economically prosperous. The annual Index of Economic Freedom states that: "The positive relationship between economic freedom and prosperity is confirmed yet again in the 2010 *Index*. Gross domestic product per capita is much higher in countries that score well in the *Index*. The positive relationship holds true at all

---

[15] The U.S. is 8th. Source:
http://heritage.org/index/pdf/2010/Index2010_ExecutiveHighlights.pdf

levels of economic freedom, but becomes even more dramatic as economic freedom increases.[16]"

So those countries are most prosperous that enjoy the greatest freedom from government intervention in the economy. That is what the research reveals, consistently year after year, in the annual Index of Economic Freedom studies. The research results show this very clearly and very consistently year in and year out. But can we explain why this is the case? There are a number of reasons, which are set out below.

<u>Public Goods and Private Goods</u>

An important distinction that must be made is the difference between public goods and private goods. The difference is as follows:

    a. <u>Private goods</u> are what we can buy at supermarkets, clothing stores, appliance stores, furniture stores, hairstyling salons, health clubs, and dry cleaners. When you think of private goods, think of anything you put in your shopping cart. We buy private goods wherever we wish, whenever we wish, and we spend whatever amount on private goods that we can afford. No-one forces us to buy private goods, so we only buy those private goods that we choose. It follows that we gain every time we purchase private goods because those purchases are completely voluntary, and we would not buy

---

[16] Source:
http://heritage.org/index/pdf/2010/Index2010_ExecutiveHighlights.pdf

anything unless we prefer that item to the money that it costs us. By the same token, sellers of private goods do not sell anything unless they prefer the money they receive for the item to the item itself. So sellers also gain every time they sell something. Otherwise they would not sell it. In short, both buyer and seller gain every time they buy or sell an item. Further, private goods are excludable and rivalrous. Excludable means that we can exclude others from enjoying that item. For example, if I buy an orange then only I can eat it, and no-one else can eat it. If I buy a recliner at the furniture store, I can sit in it and can prevent anyone else from sitting in it. It is my property, and mine alone, because I own it. No-one can be a free rider. If you want a private good, you have to pay for it. Rivalrous means that my enjoyment of the item prevents anyone else from enjoying it. For example, once I have eaten my orange, it cannot be eaten by anyone else. And once I sit in my recliner no-one else can sit in it at the same time. But public goods are the opposite of private goods.

b. <u>Public goods</u> are not what we buy at supermarkets, clothing stores, appliance stores, furniture stores, hairstyling salons, health clubs, and dry cleaners. Public goods are the U.S. military, or the justice system, (law and order, and secure property rights). Public goods may or may not be acquired voluntarily. For example, you cannot refuse to pay your income taxes because some part of those taxes is spent on the military and you are an antiwar pacifist. So it's not clear that one gains from buying public goods. Is protection from foreign attack worth what we pay for it? Most people might say yes, but there is no objective way to prove it, and it can be debated. There are many other examples of public goods that we are not free to accept or reject. For instance, just try to defy a court order, or to break the speed limit or to avoid paying your Social Security tax and see what happens. In addition public goods are not excludable. Everyone is protected from foreign attack by the U.S. military. Everyone is protected, whether they are employed by the government or employed in the private sector, or a billionaire or a pauper, or a Republican or a Democrat, or a taxpayer or a cheat. Public goods are non-excludable. Free riders cannot be excluded. Also, public goods are non-rivalrous. The fact that I enjoy protection from foreign aggression by the U.S. military does not prevent you from also enjoying protection by the very same U.S. military. And the fact that you enjoy the law and order provided by the U.S. justice system does not prevent you from also enjoying the law and order provided by the U.S. justice system.

This may be slightly unfamiliar or complex, so let's summarize the differences between public and private goods in Table 2-1 below.

	Private Goods	Public Goods
Voluntary and gainful transaction?	Voluntary gainful purchase and sale	May not be gainful or voluntary
Excludable?	Yes	No
Rivalrous?	Yes	No

Table 2-1

What does this discussion of private and public goods suggest to us? It suggests that private goods should be provided only by the private sector. And public goods must be provided by government because they cannot be provided by the private sector. Why can public goods not be provided by the private sector? For several reasons, as follows:

a. Private sector organizations should not (and probably could not) apply the coercion that must accompany some transactions in public goods.

b. Private sector organizations cannot sell items at a profit if free riders cannot be excluded from benefiting from the item without paying for it.

c. Private sector organizations cannot sell items at a profit if consumption is non-rivalrous because non-buyers can benefit just like buyers.

In summary, public goods cannot be provided in free markets because they cannot be sold for a price and at a profit. It is important to be very clear about which goods are private goods and which goods are public goods, and to avoid confusing one with the other. For example, it is easy to believe that highways must be public goods. But this would be wrong. Both throughout history and today, private roads have been financed by tolls charged to road users. People refusing to pay the toll can be excluded from use. By the same token, TV signals are not public goods. The signals can be scrambled to exclude non-payers from using the signals without paying for them. In some cases, private ownership can be a solution. Cleaning up a polluted lake, for instance, involves a free-rider problem if the lake is publicly-owned.. But if there is a private owner, however, that person can charge a user price to fishermen, boaters, recreational users, and others who benefit from the lake.

One might think that lighthouses are public goods because all ships can benefit from lighthouse signals without paying for the privilege. But this is not necessarily the case. The well-known economist, Ronald Coase [17] , found that in England there actually was a relatively efficient privately financed lighthouse system, which would refute economists' traditional statements concerning the definition of public goods. Coase found that the private owners of lighthouses contracted with the harbormasters of British ports to collect user fees from ships that were refused harbor services unless they paid lighthouse user fees. So the private lighthouse owners had devised a method of excluding free riders from the lighthouse services. They had

---

[17] Coase R. H. 'The Lighthouse in Economics' *Journal of Law and Economics*, vol. 17, no. 2, 357–76, 1974)

converted what seemed like a public good into a private good.

As we have seen, the differences between public goods and private goods can become blurred and hard to distinguish in some cases. It is not necessary to address and to attempt to solve these arcane issues here and now. It is sufficient to point out that there are a few marginal cases, but that most of the time public goods can clearly be distinguished from private goods. For our purposes that will be enough for us to proceed with the discussion.

We have established that public goods cannot be provided in free markets because they cannot be sold for a price and at a profit. That means that public goods can only be provided by the government, and not by the private sector. Just what are these essentially public goods? At a minimum the following items are generally accepted as public goods that can only be provided by government:

    a. Defense provided by our military services against attacks from foreign forces. Defense against foreign attacks is a benefit for all citizens from which no citizen can be excluded, and which is enjoyed by those who pay no taxes as well as those who do pay taxes. Defense against foreign attacks can involve coercion, such as forced compliance with a blackout by switching off all lights at night, or regulations that prohibit access to military secrets, or restricted access to military bases and military equipment. So defense against foreign attacks meets all three standards that define public goods.

b. Governments can promote economic freedom by providing a legal structure and a law-enforcement system that protect the property rights of owners and enforces contracts in an evenhanded manner. Law and order are essential for commerce to flourish and the economy to prosper. However, economic freedom also requires governments to avoid taking people's property and interfering with personal choice, voluntary exchange, and the freedom to enter and compete in labor and product markets. When governments substitute taxes, government expenditures, and regulations for personal choice, voluntary exchange, and market coordination, they reduce economic freedom. Restrictions that limit entry into occupations and business activities also reduce economic freedom. The rule of law and secure property rights provided by the criminal and civil justice systems are also generally accepted as public goods. The justice system must be able to exercise coercion in many situations. Convicted criminals must be forced to perform whatever they have been sentenced to do by the courts. Citizens must meet civic duties such as serving on juries, and the police must be authorized to use force when necessary. Further, the benefits of law and order are shared by all citizens, with none being excluded. In addition, the benefits of law and order are shared by all citizens, whether or not they pay taxes. So the rule of law and secure property rights provided by the criminal and civil justice systems are consistent with all three standards that define public goods. Of course, it should be pointed out that there are private sector forums for resolving legal disputes. For example there are "rent-a-judge" services, arbitrator organizations, and private mediation services. These private sector services do relieve some congestion in the civil courts. But they do not – and cannot – replace the civil courts because they require the consent of all parties before they can be used. A standard complaint about mediation by some parties is that the other side has not used the mediation process in a genuine attempt to settle a dispute. Rather, they have cynically used mediation to sneak a peek at the cards in their opponent's hand.

There may be a few more public goods than the two major public goods (military defense and the rule of law) described above. Be that as it may, these two named public goods must be provided by government, because they are essential to civilized life, but cannot be provided by private sector markets. So we have established that a government sector is an essential component of civilized life, and – at a minimum – this government must provide the two essential public goods described above, namely (a) the national military force to protect citizens from foreign aggression, and (b) the rule of law and secure property rights. This leaves at least two more questions about what should be done in the public sector and what should be done in the private sector, and why:

    a. Should the government be restricted to providing only public goods?
    b. What should the private sector provide,

Should the government be restricted to providing only public goods?

It has already been shown that government has vital functions to perform in the economy by providing military defense and the rule of law. Why should government not go much further and provide many more goods? That would certainly be the view of socialism, communism and fascism. But there many good reasons to reject this view. Here are the main reasons why government should be strictly restricted to providing public goods only, and prohibited from providing private goods.

    1. The Agency Problem: An agency relationship arises whenever one or more individuals, called principals, hire one or more other individuals, called agents, to perform some service and then delegate decision-making authority to the agents. One example of an agency relationship is when voters elect a politician to represent them in the legislature. The voters are the principals and the elected legislator is the agent. Another example of an agency relationship is when investors elect directors to the board of a corporation to represent their corporation. These relationships are not necessarily agreeable In fact, agency theory

is concerned with conflicts of interest between agents and principals. When agency conflict takes place it also tends to give rise to agency costs, which are expenses incurred in order to promote an effective agency relationship (for example, offering management performance bonuses to encourage managers to act in the shareholders' interests). Agency theory suggests that, in imperfect labor and capital markets, agents will seek to maximize their own interests rather than the interests of the principals who the agents are supposed to represent. Agents have the ability to operate in their own self-interest rather than in the best interests of their principals because of asymmetric information (which means that agents know the inside information better than their principals). Evidence of self-interested agent behavior includes special perquisites (such as lavish, expense-account overseas trips and rich retirement benefits and Cadillac healthcare plans for politicians). Agency theory tells us that agents like politicians will tend to follow their individual best interests, rather than doing their duty to represent the interests of their principals. This is probably no surprise to anyone. It means that government activities are more likely to serve the interests of politicians than the interests of the public. So that is one reason not to entrust any more tasks to government than absolutely necessary.

2 <u>Skin In The Game</u>: Milton Friedman is famous for saying that people are a great deal more careful in spending their own money than in spending other peoples' money. When we spend our own money, we have skin in the game. But when spending other peoples' money, government has no skin in the game. In the public sector, government is always spending the taxpayers' money, and is never spending the personal money of politicians. In the private sector, every firm and every consumer is spending their own money. So private sector parties have skin in the game, but governments do not have skin in the game. That is one more reason not to entrust any more tasks to government than absolutely necessary.

3. <u>Innovation Versus Inertia</u>: In the private sector successful innovators are well rewarded, as for example Steve Jobs of Apple Computer, Bill Gates of Microsoft, and Warren Buffett, to name just three well-known innovators. At the same time, failures are severely punished. For example, once-famous auto makes such as Oldsmobile, Pontiac, Plymouth, and Saturn have become extinct. Well-known firms like Merrill Lynch, Bear Sterns and Lehman are no longer flourishing entities but have been liquidated or absorbed by other corporations. However in government programs it is hard to name any successful innovations. But failures are seldom, if ever, liquidated or

terminated. For example, the War on Poverty was started by then-president Lyndon Johnson in the 1960's. Today in 2010 poverty is still with us more than 40 years later. Despite its failure to eliminate poverty, the War on Poverty program remains in force. Fannie Mae and Freddie Mac are both colossal failures. But both have been bailed out at huge cost by our government and remain in business rather than being liquidated. It seems that there are few rewards for success or penalties for failure in government. Incentives for success and penalties for failure are powerful and important factors that are prominent in the private sector, but seemingly absent in the government sector. That is yet one more reason not to entrust any more tasks to government than absolutely necessary.

4.   Public Versus Private Ownership: A well-known situation in economics is known as "The Tragedy Of The Commons." The Tragedy Of The Commons[18] refers to the recurring devastation of common (i.e., not privately owned) pastures in England. It was asked: "Why are the cattle on a common so puny and stunted? Why is the common itself so bare-worn, and cropped so differently from the adjoining enclosures?" The answer was that each person exploiting the common was driven by self-interest. At the stage when the carrying capacity of the commons

---

[18] See
http://www.econlib.org/library/Enc/TragedyoftheCommons.html

was exhausted, a herdsman might ask if he should add another animal to his herd? Because the herdsman owned his animals, the gain of doing so would come only to him. But the loss suffered by overloading the pasture would be shared among all the herdsmen. Because the privatized gain would exceed his share of the joint loss, a self-seeking herdsman would add another animal to his herd. And another and yet another, *ad infinitum*. And so would all the other herdsmen as well. Ultimately, the common property would be ruined. The point of "The Tragedy Of The Commons" is that public ownership is ineffective in the care and maintenance of an economic resource. Public ownership means that no-one acts as an owner. In other words, every economic resource must meet the challenge of human self-interest. An unmanaged commons in a world of limited material wealth and unlimited desires inevitably ends in ruin. Inevitable ruin is what justifies the label of "tragedy." Another example of a government-created tragedy of the commons is congestion on public roads that do not charge tolls. If roads were privately owned, owners would charge tolls and people would take the toll into account in deciding whether to use them. Owners of private roads would probably also engage in what is called peak-load pricing. This means charging higher prices during times of peak demand and lower prices at other times. But because governments own roads that they finance with tax dollars, they normally do not charge tolls. The government makes roads into a commons. The result is congestion. There are many examples of "The Tragedy Of The Commons." One is over-fished oceans, and another is the hunting of endangered species on public lands. As the example of congested roads shows, private ownership is the solution to all instances of "The Tragedy Of The Commons." Private ownership is not compatible with government (or public) ownership. That is yet one more reason not to entrust any more tasks to government than absolutely necessary.

5. Crony capitalism: the divide between socialism (government ownership of the means of production) and capitalism (private ownership of the means of production) is sometimes blurred by crony capitalism. Crony capitalism takes place when large companies receive favored treatment from government in exchange for large campaign contributions for politicians. It is very tempting for large companies to seek favors from government. As Adam Smith pointed out: *"People of the same trade seldom meet together, even for merriment and diversion, but the conversation ends in a conspiracy against the public, or in some contrivance to raise prices.... But though the law cannot hinder people of the same trade from sometimes assembling together, it ought to do nothing to facilitate such assemblies,*

much less to render them necessary[19]. It is also very tempting to politicians to exact large campaign contributions in exchange for granting political favors. Therefore outbreaks of crony capitalism are likely to occur. It is important to understand that crony capitalism is incompatible with the rule of law, which requires equal treatment for all, whether or not well-connected, and where no-one should be above the law. Crony capitalism is also incompatible with free enterprise and competitive markets. Crony capitalism renders favors to well-connected competitors over unconnected competitors, and prevents free and open competition. Clearly crony capitalism is by no means free enterprise, and represents a conspiracy between large companies and government to subvert and defeat the rule of law and competitive markets. The prevention of crony capitalism depends on a clear understanding that it represents improper government interference in the private sector for no valid economic reason, and only because both the government officials and the company officials involved have ignored their responsibilities as agents and have failed to do their duty towards their principals[20]. That is yet one more reason not

---

[19] In his book "The Wealth of Nations" published in 1776. These concerns are as pressing today as they were back in 1776.

[20] Namely the voters in the case of politicians, and the investors in the case of company officials.

to entrust any more tasks to government than absolutely necessary.

6. "Do Something!" When any kind of crisis takes place, there arises a call from some members of the public for government to "do something." Often this call comes from a special interest group that seeks a favor from government. Politicians are eager to "do something" because a crisis presents an opportunity to seize more power that would not otherwise be available. Therefore politicians tend to regard crises as opportunities that should not be wasted but should be exploited. The call to "do something" is usually based on appealing slogans, rather than careful consideration of the facts in order to determine how successful government interventions in the economy have been in the past, in similar situations. Often, government programs are undertaken with the best of intentions, even if they end up with the worst of results. In testimony before the U.S. Congress earlier this year a witness stated that: "Given ... the proven good economic results in countries around the world that respect principles of economic freedom and market-based decision-making, I would submit that the first responsibility of policy makers in leading economies, especially in a time of downturn or crisis, is to preserve the capitalist system and to do no harm. Markets are by and large self-correcting. Government interventions, which are almost always designed to restore or protect the status quo

ante, impede the corrective action of the market and thus slow recovery. [21] " It has been shown in numerous studies that government interference in the economy is more apt to aggravate crises than to help solve problems. Adam Smith was no admirer of politicians. He wrote: "insidious and crafty animal, vulgarly called a statesman or politician[22]" Examples of the dismal failure of government intervention are very numerous – here are just a few:

- "Grants or subsidized loans subvert the motivation for private self-protection. For example, subsidized government flood insurance induces excessive construction in areas that are vulnerable to flooding[23]."
- "We do have at least two natural experiments in which a single nation was bisected by very different forms of governments: the two Germanys from the end of World War II to reunification in 1991, and the two Koreas. In both cases, the government that allowed private property and free (at least compared with its counterpart government) enterprise oversaw an economic "miracle," while the more totalitarian

---

[21] Source:
http://www.heritage.org/research/testimony/government-intervention-a-threat-to-economic-recovery
[22] Adam Smith, "The Wealth of Nations" 1776.
[23] Source:
http://www.econlib.org/library/Enc/DisasterandRecovery.html

governments in the pairings each produced decades of stagnation and poverty. [24]". In each case, both the people and the respective situations were similar before the parts were split. This is as close as we can ever get to a laboratory experiment in the real world. That fact makes these findings significant

- "As in the case of other price ceilings, rent control causes shortages, diminution in the quality of the product, and queues. [25] ."'Several decades of studies using aggregate time-series data from a variety of countries have found that minimum wage laws reduce employment. At current U.S. wage levels, estimates of job losses suggest that a 10 percent in crease in the minimum wage would decrease employment of low-skilled workers by 1 or 2 percent. The job losses for black U.S. teenagers have been found to be even greater, presumably because, on average, they have fewer skills. [26]" This article from the New York Times illustrates the loss of

---

[24] Source: http://www.econlib.org/library/Enc/EmpiricsofEconomicGrowth.html
[25] Source: http://www.econlib.org/library/Enc/RentControl.html
[26] Source: http://www.econlib.org/library/Enc/MinimumWages.html

jobs caused by the minimum wage[27]: "NEWCASTLE, South Africa — The sheriff arrived at the factory here to shut it down, part of a national enforcement drive against clothing manufacturers who violate the minimum wage. But women working on the factory floor — the supposed beneficiaries of the crackdown — clambered atop cutting tables and ironing boards to raise anguished cries against it. "Why? Why?" shouted Nokuthula Masango, 25, after the authorities carted away bolts of gaily colored fabric. She made just $36 a week, $21 less than the minimum wage, but needed the meager pay to help support a large extended family that includes her five unemployed siblings and their children. The women's spontaneous protest is just one sign of how acute South Africa's long-running unemployment crisis has become. With their own industry in ruinous decline, the victim of low-wage competition from China, and too few unskilled jobs being created in South Africa, the women feared being out of work more than getting stuck in poorly paid jobs. "

---

[27] Source:
http://www.nytimes.com/2010/09/27/world/africa/27safrica.html?_r=2&hp

- Politics has been described as "the art of the possible." More aptly, it should be described as "the art of the impossible." For example, the U.S. government professes to make us energy-independent, so that we no longer need to import 66% of our oil. But at the same time our government bans drilling for oil offshore and in the ANWAR area of Alaska – which makes it impossible to make us energy-independent. Another example is our government's strenuous efforts to provide "affordable housing" to people without sufficient cash to pay a reasonable deposit and to afford monthly mortgage payments. Despite all desires to achieve this worthy goal, it has led only to a serious housing crisis rather than to "affordable housing." There are countless more examples of politicians promising impossible results, and then failing to deliver the intended results (but succeeding in the politician's own goals of getting elected or re-elected).

We have supplied many reasons not to entrust any more tasks to government than absolutely necessary. So it is clear that government should be strictly limited to providing public goods, and should not be involved in any fashion at all in the provision of private goods. Government interference in free enterprise does damage rather than good. Next, it is time to consider the adequacy of the private sector in serving private goods. How well do free markets function, and are there cases of market failure? That question is addressed in Chapter 3.

Chapter Summary

The main points of Chapter 2 are as follows:

1. In practice, virtually all economies are mixed, with some activities carried out by the government, and other activities carried out in the private sector. So the issue of government sector and private sector becomes which economic activities should be performed by government, and which economic activities should be performed in the private sector?
2. The countries that enjoy the most economic freedom from government intervention are the most economically prosperous. The countries that enjoy the least economic freedom from government intervention are the least economically prosperous.
3. Private goods should be provided only by the private sector. And public goods must be provided by government because they cannot be provided by the private sector.
4. It has been shown that government has vital functions to perform in the economy by providing military defense and the rule of law. Why should government not go much further and provide many more goods? That

would certainly be the view of socialism, communism and fascism. But there many good reasons to reject this view.

5. Reasons why government should provide only public goods include:

    a. The agency problem.

    b. The "skin in the game" issue.

    c. Private sector innovation versus public sector inertia.

    d. The tragedy of the commons problem.

    e. The drift towards crony capitalism.

    f. The urge to "do something!"

    g. The repeated failure of well-intended government programs.

6. Government interference in free enterprise does damage rather than good. Next, in Chapter 3 we will consider the adequacy of the private sector in providing private goods.

Chapter 3

What the Private Sector Should Do

The inherent vice of capitalism is the unequal sharing of blessings; the inherent virtue of socialism is the equal sharing of miseries.
Winston Churchill

Introduction

The private sector is defined as the part of the economy that is not controlled by government. That definition may be too simple considering that some firms are privately owned, but are still to some extent controlled by government because they are regulated by government agencies. So we need to clarify our definition to shed more light on this issue. In Chapter 2 we concluded that government should be confined to doing only what cannot be done in the private sector. That means that government should not be regulating any activity in the private sector – subject only to one exception. That exception is government enforcement of the rule of law, including secure property rights. Therefore government regulation should go no further than enforcement of the rule of law, including secure property rights. Inherently the rule of law must treat all equally, without favoritism, so that no-one is above the law. In essence, government is always to be the referee in the private sector, and never a player. That is a bright line, and should never be crossed.

The private sector therefore includes all economic activity, within the rule of law, which is not controlled by government. Essentially the private sector consists of markets, where users and suppliers buy and sell private goods and services. It is readily conceded that markets are not perfect. There will sometimes be imperfections such as frictional unemployment[28] or occasional disruptions in supply or demand. Sometimes these imperfections are called "market failure." Interventionist politicians usually allege market failure to justify their interventions. Economists have identified the following main types of market failure:

- The abuse of market power which may transpire when a single seller (monopoly) or buyer (monopsony) can exert significant influence over price or quantity sold. The abuse of market power is usually dealt with by criminal prosecution or civil suit under the antitrust laws. Therefore it tends to be a temporary rather than a long-lasting problem and is usually solved by the courts.

- Externalities when the action of one party imposes a positive benefit or a negative cost on outsiders. For example, the benefit a neighbor enjoys from your rose garden, or the negative costs imposed on neighbors by

---

[28] Frictional unemployment is caused by unemployed workers in transition from one job to another or from one career to another. Frictional unemployment is distinguished from structural unemployment (due to relocation or bankruptcy of a company or technical progress or changes in consumer taste), or cyclical unemployment (due to economic downturn or recession).

a firm polluting the environment. Negative externalities also tend to be temporary rather than long-lasting problems, and are usually solved by the courts.

- Where there is incomplete or asymmetric information or uncertainty. Asymmetric information exists when one party to a transaction has information that the other party cannot share. For example, many people will not buy a used car because the seller knows its defects but the buyer does not, and it is difficult or expensive for the buyer to obtain the missing information. In cases of asymmetric information it is often best for the uninformed party to avoid the transaction, bearing in mind the wise saying "buyer beware." In cases of incomplete information, the rule of law is useful in solving the problem by requiring full disclosure. Examples are the mandatory disclosures of product ingredients, and truth in advertising, both of which are required under the rule of law.

Therefore most cases of "market failure" are temporary in nature and of short duration. This contrasts sharply with government intervention, which often results from the "do something" impulse and frequently ends in government failures. [29] The lesson to be drawn is that accusations of "market failure" should be viewed with skepticism, and should be recognized as likely

---

[29] As described by the many examples of government failure listed in Chapter 2.

pretexts for government to "do something" which is liable in turn to result in government failure.

Our conclusion is that markets are by no means perfect. Economics correctly states that markets tend towards equilibrium – which means that markets may be imperfect, but lean towards correcting their imperfections. In contrast, government failures tend to turn into enduring problems, such as our current housing crisis, the ongoing but unsuccessful thirty-year "war on poverty" and the chronic federal budget deficits. With their faults, free markets are wealth-producing, as explained below.

Wealth-Producing Free Markets

When you or I buy any private good we do so voluntarily. We would not buy the good or service in question unless we want it more than the money we pay for it. Clearly we would not buy anything unless we want it more than the money we pay for it. By the same token, the voluntary seller would not sell the good or service in question unless they want the money we pay more than the good or service itself. Clearly sellers would not sell anything unless they want the money we pay for it more than the good or service itself. So, in every transaction, both the buyer and the seller benefit. There is no loser because everyone involved is a winner. In other words, all transactions in private goods are wealth-producing for all parties involved. Since free markets make everyone better-off, they are wealth-producing. All voluntary transactions are wealth-producing, but the same cannot be said for transactions involving coercion.

All free market transactions are voluntary and therefore wealth-producing. But transactions involving government are not necessarily voluntary, because government has coercive power. Therefore transactions involving government are not necessarily wealth-producing. When given the choice we should always prefer wealth-producing transactions over transactions that are not necessarily wealth-producing. That means all transactions are best done in the free market private sector, rather than by government. The only exceptions are for public goods, which must be supplied by government because they cannot be supplied by the private sector free market. This is not the only reason for favoring the private sector whenever possible. Further reasons are set out below.

Skin In The Game

As we wrote in Chapter 2, Milton Friedman is famous for saying that people are a great deal more careful in spending their own money than in spending other peoples' money. When we spend our own money, we have skin in the game. But when spending other peoples' money, government has no skin in the game. In the public sector, government is always spending the taxpayers' money, and is never spending the personal money of politicians. In the private sector, every firm and every consumer is spending their own money. So private sector parties have skin in the game, but governments do not have skin in the game.

In the private sector successful firms make money because they are rewarded for providing goods and services that people want to buy. They have a powerful incentive to do good because then they do well by making profits. Unsuccessful firms lose their own money, not public money. That is a powerful incentive to avoid blunders, because blunders create losses and losses can lead to bankruptcy. Here is one more reason to entrust economic tasks to the private sector rather than the government sector. More reasons follow below.

Unintended Consequences

Often the best of intentions can turn out to have unforeseen consequences. The principle of unintended consequences provides the basis for many criticisms of government programs. As the critics see it, unintended consequences can add so much to the costs of some programs that they make the programs unwise even if they achieve their stated goals. For instance, the U.S. government has imposed quotas on imports of steel in order to protect steel companies and steelworkers from lower-priced steel imports. The quotas did help steel companies. But they also made less of the cheap steel available to U.S. automakers. As a result, the automakers had to pay more for steel than their foreign competitors did. So a policy that intended to protect the domestic steel industry from foreign competition made it harder for the domestic auto industry to compete with imports.

People outraged about high prices of plywood in areas devastated by hurricanes, for example, may advocate price controls to prevent price gouging.

An unintended consequence is that plywood suppliers outside the region, who would be willing to provide plywood quickly at a higher market price, are less willing to do so at the government-controlled price. This creates a shortage of plywood where it is badly needed.

The current housing crisis was caused by government insistence on "affordable housing" by making mortgage loans to home buyers who could not afford the customary down payments or monthly mortgage installments. There are very many examples of unintended consequences. Rather than taking more time to cite them, we simply observe that the future is unknown and unknowable, that foresight is prone to error, and unintended consequences are extremely common. Therefore unintended consequences can add so much to the costs of some government programs that they make the programs unwise. Of course, unintended consequences can also occur in the private sector. But in this case private firms lose their own money, unlike government programs where consequences unintended by politicians lose the taxpayers' money.

Centralized Decision Making.

Communism, socialism and fascism all are dedicated to centralized decision-making by the few officials at the top. In contrast, capitalism is characterized by decentralized decision-making by individuals regardless of whether they are at the top or the bottom or any other place. Under centralized decision-making by the few officials at the top, it is quite impossible to know what kinds of goods and services are needed, and in what quantities each kind of goods and services are needed. Not only are economies far too complex to be masterminded by the few officials at the top, but the necessary information is simply missing, and the required calculations are overwhelming. It is hard enough for a Wal-Mart or a Costco to keep its thousands of items of merchandise well-stocked, well-balanced, and well-organized, let alone to manage total supply and demand for an entire economy. Just to take a simple example, consider men's dress shirts, as shown in Table 3-1 below:

Feature:	Choices:	Number of Choices
Cloth	Cotton Broadcloth, Synthetic, Blend	3
Style	Slim Fit, Regular, Loose	3
Fit	Big, Regular, Tall	3
Neck Size	15" to 18" in half-inch steps	7
Sleeve Length	Short Sleeve, Long Sleeve 32"-35"	5
Color	Solid: White, Light Blue, Dark Blue, Grey, Green, Pink, Yellow, Black. Stripe: Narrow, Wide, Regular. Check: Large, Small.	13
Collar	Pointed, Long Pointed, Wide V, Banded	4

Table 3-1

As Table 3-1 shows, men's dress shirts come in varieties of cloth, style, fit, neck size, sleeve length, color and type of collar. If we multiply the number of choices in each feature, we get 3 x 3 x 3 x7 x5 x 13 x 4 = 49,140 different choices. So a store would need to stock 49,140 men's dress shirts if it wanted to have just one of each type in its inventory. But say that a store decided to keep 20 of its most popular types of men's dress shirts in its inventory. Then the results would be a far greater number than 49,140. So just one simple example of a men's dress shirt reveals the complexity involved in planning the production, distribution and consumption of goods. Consider that an average supermarket stocks almost 50,000 different items[30]. That gives some idea of the complexity faced by central planners in determining production, distribution and consumption of goods and services in a communist or socialist economy.

Therefore it is no surprise that every communist, socialist, and fascist economy has been a serious disaster. Until China and Russia dropped major components of their communist ideology, they were economic failures unable to feed, shelter or clothe their citizens. Under socialism India remained mired in poverty until much of its socialism was eradicated – and economic progress then ensued. To this day nations like North Korea, Cuba, Zimbabwe and other nations labor and suffer privation under the yoke of communism, socialism and fascism.

In a few circles it remains fashionable to favor communism or socialism, especially when those circles are safely located among the luxuries of capitalism. Evading the burden of living under the

---

[30] Source:
http://www.fmi.org/facts_figs/?fuseaction=superfact

grinding poverty of communism or socialism, critics of capitalism can safely (if hypocritically) enjoy both the creature comforts of capitalism and the self-serving theoretical allegiance to communist or socialist concepts. Simple logic should tell us that a few top officials in communist or socialist economies cannot possibly match the innovative talents of thousands of gifted individuals in free societies. In free societies a Steve Jobs or a Bill Gates or a Warren Buffett or a Donald Trump can come out of nowhere with a great idea and be rewarded richly for their creative contributions.

As Adam Smith observed "It is not from the benevolence of the butcher, or the baker, that we expect our dinner, but from regard to their own self interest. [31] " Under communism or socialism or fascism there are no rewards or incentives for self interest, so in those societies it is only from the benevolence of the butcher, or the baker, that we expect our dinner. Naturally, relying only upon the benevolence of strangers is risky or even foolhardy. In that case, the dinner is more likely to be absent than present.

Spontaneous Order Versus Rules and Plans

Under communism or socialism or fascism the state owns or regulates all the means of production. All production is under the orders of government officials, and ultimately an autocrat of some kind. But under free enterprise no-one is in charge of production. There is only spontaneous order, or – if you like – a self-organizing system. That raises the

---

[31] In "The Wealth of Nations" published in 1776.

question of how can spontaneous order function without supervision, or how can a system without a head organize itself? Adam Smith called this phenomenon an "invisible hand" and generations of students since have hoped that the invisible hand might strangle its invisible throat! But seriously, how does this "invisible hand" actually work?

Bear in mind that self-organizing systems are neither rare nor unusual. Familiar examples of self-organizing systems are as follows:

1. The gulfstream in the Atlantic Ocean.
2. The ocean tides.
3. The seasons of summer, autumn, winter, and spring.
4. The solar system.
5. The weather.
6. The human digestive system.
7. The human circulatory system
8. The human brain.
9. The rain forest.
10. The evolution of species.
11. Hurricanes.
12. A beehive.
13. An ant colony.
14. Bird migration.
15. Salmon spawning.

None of the above examples of self-organizing systems have a manager or chief to direct activities. Nevertheless they function in an organized manner with regularity but without a manager to make decisions or give directions.

In the case of economic systems a perfect example is the well-know article entitled "I, Pencil"[32] written by Leonard E. Read. It is the autobiography of an ordinary number 2 lead pencil, which we are told no-one knows how to make, yet is in plentiful supply and easy to buy. No-one knows how to make a plain wooden pencil because they would need to master all the following tasks:

1. Locate cedars of straight grain that grow in Northern California and Oregon.
2. Be able to use all the saws and trucks and rope and the countless other gear used in harvesting and carting the cedar logs to the railroad siding.
3. Possess the skills involved in the mining of ore, the making of steel and its refinement into saws, axes, motors; the growing of hemp and bringing it through all the stages to heavy and strong rope; the logging camps with their beds and mess halls, the cookery and the raising of all the foods.
4. Be able to make flat cars and rails and railroad engines and to construct and install the related communication systems.
5. Cut the cedar logs into small, pencil-length slats less than one-fourth of an inch in thickness.
6. Ensure that these slats are kiln dried and then tinted.
7. Make sure that the slats are waxed and kiln dried again.
8. Possess the skills that go into the making of the tint and the kilns, into supplying the heat,

---

[32] http://fee.org/library/books/i-pencil-2/

the light and power, the belts, motors, and all the other things a mill requires.

9. Be able to pour the concrete for the dam of the electric utility company hydro plant which supplies the mill's power.

10. Be competent in selling the cedar slats to the pencil factory.

These 10 steps merely get the slats as far as the pencil company. We have not yet considered the graphite that provides the lead in the pencil, the glue that keeps the lead inside the cedar slats, the rubber for the eraser tip, and the tin ferrule that attaches the eraser to the pencil. We have not even started to locate where the graphite, the glue, the rubber or the tin ferrule can be obtained, and the processes required to produce these pencil components and to get them to the pencil factory. We have also not yet described how the pencils are put together, sold to distributors, transported to stores or sold to users. But we have given a quick impression of how many steps need to be completed to make a simple lead pencil. We have illustrated why no one person could possibly know nearly enough to make a plain wooden lead pencil. Yet these pencils get made and get sold in vast numbers to millions of children, students, workers and other people who use pencils.

How is this miracle accomplished? The answer is through the price system. At every step in the many stages of creating pencils, each firm involved needs only to what prices they must pay to obtain raw materials, what costs are incurred in manufacturing the product, what prices can be charged for the finished product, and what profit can be made from these activities. The price system is what enables each step in making a pencil to be successfully completed even though no-one knows how to make a pencil, and even though the firms at each step may be strangers to each other, and even though the price system has no leader or director. In short, the price system is what makes the entire free enterprise economy function. If you like, the price system is the DNA that enables the invisible hand to work its invisible miracle.

It is the free market price system that enables a capitalist economy to function. In a communist or socialist economy there is no price system, because all decisions are made by the central planners at the top. The communist or socialist economy has no price system to guide its decisions, it has no invisible hand, and no self-organizing system. In short the communist or socialist economy has to stumble as best it can in the dark. That is why the communist or socialist economy is clumsy, and unable to produce economic progress or prosperity.

It is the price system that lets the free enterprise capitalist economy function with the precision of a Swiss watch – even though there is no watchmaker. There is only a self-organizing system that automatically creates spontaneous order. The free enterprise private sector self-organizing system is just like other self-organizing systems, such as the ocean tides, the seasons, the blood circulatory system, and a beehive.

And that is why all economic activity possible should be pursued in the private sector. Remember that the government sector has no price system, and has to stumble as best it can in the dark, clumsily and inefficiently. These are yet more reasons why economic activity is best performed in the private sector as far as possible, and why the government should not interfere with the economy, either by owning and operating the means of production, or attempting to regulate economic activity in the private sector.

<u>Monopoly Or Competition.</u>

Adam Smith wrote his famous passage: ""It is not from the benevolence of the butcher, or the baker, that we expect our dinner, but from regard to their own self interest.[33]" But self interest alone does not guarantee our dinner. There must also be competition. If the butcher or the baker is a monopolist, with no competitors, then he will charge whatever the traffic will bear. Without doubt, the monopoly price will be higher than the competitive price. Therefore it is competition that keeps the price of our dinner reasonable.

Once there is competition, firms have to vie with each other for customers. In order to win and retain customers firms must do the following things:

1. Charge competitive prices.
2. Deal honestly and reasonably with customers.
3. Disclose important information and not hide product defects or mislead customers.
4. Observe ethical standards with customers, suppliers, employees and government agencies.

---

[33] In "The Wealth of Nations" published in 1776.

Failure to do these things can fool customers, suppliers, employees and government agencies for a while, but sooner or later the truth will leak out. As Abraham Lincoln pointed out, "You can fool some of the people all of the time, and all of the people some of the time, but you can not fool all of the people all of the time." Therefore it is competition that ensures ethical conduct. It is competition that keeps self-interest different and distinct from selfishness. Selfishness is putting oneself first, to the detriment of others. But enlightened self-interest is putting others first, rather than putting only oneself first. The result is that free enterprise capitalism with free competition is inherently moral. Whether or not people are inclined to be ethical, they have every incentive to behave in a moral manner. But monopoly lacks the incentive for ethical behavior. That is why free enterprise capitalism is a moral system, but why monopoly is not a moral system. The government sector is a monopoly, because there is only one government in any jurisdiction. Government is not a competitive enterprise – it is by definition a monopoly.

When transactions are entered into in the competitive free enterprise private sector, they tend to be moral in nature. But when transactions are entered into in the government sector, they are under a monopoly. Unfortunately monopoly lacks the incentive for ethical behavior. That is another reason that all economic activity possible should be pursued in the private sector, and not in the government sector.

Economics is a strange subject. On the one hand, it is complex and requires deep study in order to fully understand it. In this characteristic it is just like rocket science, brain surgery or nuclear physics. On the other hand, people who would never dream of discussing rocket science, brain surgery or nuclear physics seem to have no hesitation in confidently making economic pronouncements despite being just as ignorant about economics as they are about rocket science, brain surgery or nuclear physics. Probably this is because politicians make important decisions that have serious economic implications. Although most politicians have little if any understanding of economics, they tend to discuss economic issues with an outward confidence that is totally unwarranted. Therefore it is probably the glib pronouncements on economic issues of politicians that give individuals the false idea that anyone can speak authoritatively on economics without education, training or experience in economics. That brings us to the subject of our next chapter, which is common economic fallacies.

Chapter Summary

The main points of Chapter 3 are as follows:

This chapter examined some reasons why all economic activity possible should be pursued in the private sector, and not in the government sector. These reasons are as follows:

1. Wealth production. Economic transactions in the free enterprise private sector are wealth-producing for all parties, which is

not necessarily the case in the government sector.

2. Skin in the game. In the private sector parties win or lose with their own money. They are prudent because they have skin in the game. In the government sector parties use other people's (the taxpayers') money. They are reckless because they have no skin in the game.

3. Unintended consequences. Many programs have the best of motives, but result in adverse unintended consequences. In the private sector, firms are rewarded for success and penalized for failure, which puts a premium on caution and good sense. In the government sector politicians are not held to account for unintended consequences of foolhardy policies. Since there are no penalties for failure, there is little incentive for politicians to exercise caution and good sense.

4. Centralized Decision Making. Communism, socialism and fascism all are rigidly dedicated to centralized decision-making by the few officials at the top. In sharp contrast, capitalism is characterized by decentralized decision-making by individuals regardless of whether they are at the top or the bottom or any other place. The few officials at the top are no match for the most innovative and entrepreneurial individuals in an entire country. Therefore it is no surprise that every communist, socialist, and fascist economy has been a serious disaster. Until China and Russia dropped major components of their communist ideology,

they were economic failures unable to feed, shelter or clothe their citizens.

5. Spontaneous Order Versus Rules and Plans. It is the price system that lets the free enterprise capitalist economy function spontaneously but with the precision of a Swiss watch – even though there is no watchmaker. There is only a self-organizing system that automatically creates spontaneous order. The free enterprise private sector self-organizing system is just like other self-organizing systems, such as the ocean tides, the seasons, the blood circulatory system, and a beehive. No government can possible outperform the spontaneous, self-organizing free enterprise market.

6. Monopoly Or Competition. When transactions are entered into in the competitive free enterprise private sector, they tend to be moral in nature. But when transactions are entered into in the government sector, they are under a monopoly. Unfortunately monopoly lacks the incentive for ethical behavior. That is another reason that all economic activity possible should be pursued in the private sector, and not in the government sector.

The reasons summarized above are why all economic activity possible should be pursued in the private sector. These are yet more reasons why economic activity is best performed in the private sector as far as possible, and why the government should not interfere with the economy, either by owning and operating the means of production, or attempting to regulate economic activity in the private sector. But it is not necessary to belabor the point any further because that would only be repetition – this solution has already been demonstrated many times over.

Chapter 4

Common Economic Fallacies

If you're not a liberal *at twenty you have no heart, if you're not a* conservative *at forty you have no brain.*
Winston Churchill

Introduction

People who would never venture to express an opinion on rocket science or brain surgery or nuclear physics have no hesitation in confidently making pronouncements on major, complex economic issues. These confident pronouncements are usually in error, but seldom in doubt. The purpose of this chapter is to help people to avoid this pitfall by understanding a few key things, as follows:

1. Economics is not a matter of subjective guesswork or personal opinion. It is the product of logic, factual evidence, and careful analysis in order to obtain results that are objective, verifiable, and able to survive any test or challenge. Economics is not superficial or cursory or trivial. It is not a spectator sport. Its principles are developed only by meticulous research, thorough investigation and profound deliberation. Economics requires years of education, study, experience and dedication – just like becoming an expert in rocket science or brain surgery or nuclear physics.

2. Economics deals with what is seen, and what is not seen. Here is an example[34]. Imagine that kids are playing baseball in the street. One of them hits the ball hard and it breaks a window in a nearby house. A passer-by says: "Well, that's a pity. But its not all bad. At least the local hardware store will sell some glass and some putty. In fact, how would that hardware store make a living unless a window was broken once in a while?" He concludes that an occasional broken window helps the economy. That is what is seen. But what is unseen? What is unseen is that the owner of the house will need to pay for replacing the broken window. So that owner will have less money to spend on something else. Maybe she will be unable to buy that new pair of shoes she was planning on purchasing. Once we consider what is unseen, we realize that the economy will not benefit from that window repair. The extra business from the broken window will be offset by the lost business from the shoes that will not be purchased. The lesson is to always look beyond what is seen, and also to consider what may not be seen. In other words, we need to go further than the obvious and the superficial in order to see the whole picture.

If we bear these two factors in mind, perhaps we can avoid being taken in by the common fallacies described below.

---

[34] http://www.econlib.org/library/Bastiat/basEss1.html

Common Fallacies

1.   Price Controls Are Effective. Ever since the earliest times governments have been trying to set maximum or minimum prices. The Old Testament banned interest on loans to fellow Israelites. In the Middle Ages governments fixed the maximum price of bread. In more modern years, governments in the United States have fixed the maximum price of gasoline, the maximum rent on apartments in New York City and San Francisco, and the minimum wage of unskilled labor, to name just a few examples of price control floors and ceilings. These price controls have a superficial appeal as necessary restrictions to protect consumers and workers from greedy oil companies, landlords, and business owners. That is what is seen. But what is unseen is that price ceilings prevent prices from exceeding a set maximum, which leads to shortages. Price floors forbid prices below a certain minimum, and cause surpluses. Imagine that the supply and demand for eggs are balanced at the present price, and that the government then fixes a lower maximum price. The supply of eggs will decrease, but the demand for eggs will increase. The outcome will be extra demand but lower supply. Some consumers will benefit by purchasing eggs at the lower price, but others will be forced to go without eggs.

Price controls prevent the price system from rationing the available supply. So some other mechanism must take its place. Long waiting lines are one prospect. When the United States set maximum prices for gasoline in the 1970's, and drivers had to wait in long lines to buy gasoline, experiencing a sample of life in the Soviet Union.

The true price of gasoline included both the cash paid and the time spent waiting in line. Some unscrupulous gas stations made drivers purchase tires or accessories in order to get gas. Other gas stations sold gas at illegally high prices on the black market. Evasion of the price control regulations tempted people into many subterfuges. But as soon as the price control was lifted, the long waiting lines disappeared, and the evasions ceased.

Similarly, rent controls led to subterfuges. Tenants planning to move demanded "key money" as bribes to turn over their homes to new tenants.. Landlords reduced their maintenance of rent-controlled apartments. And landlords stopped building new homes – thus creating shortages of rental accommodations. The minimum wage often prices low-skilled workers out of the labor market. Employers typically are not willing to pay an unskilled worker more than the value of the additional product that he produces. An unskilled youth who produces $5.00 worth of goods in an hour will have a very difficult time finding a job if he must be paid $7.00 an hour. Minimum wage laws are frequently pursued by labor unions who wish to get rid of the competition of low-paid non-union workers. Research has consistently shown that minimum wages create unemployment for the very people they are designed to help – unskilled workers.

The surface appeal of price controls is based upon what is seen. But what is unseen is that they seldom work as planned, and tend to lead to shortages, surpluses and subterfuges.

2. The Decline of U.S. Manufacturing.

It is widely believed that U.S. manufacturing has been in decline for many years, and is likely to die in the near future. But the actual figures tell a very different story. Here in Table 4-1 are the annual figures for value added to GDP by the U.S. manufacturing industry, as reported by the U.S. Government Bureau of Economic Analysis[35]:

Year	$billions
1998	1,326.7
1999	1368.1
2000	1,415.6
2001	1,343.9
2002	1,355.5
2003	1,374.0
2004	1,482.7
2005	1,568.0
2006	1,651.5
2007	1,708.6
2008	1,669.6
2009	1,568.6

Table 4-1

Table 4-1 clearly shows that U.S. manufacturing is not only alive, but actually grew in most years since 1998. The average annual rate of growth from 1998 through 2009 was 1.53%. In fact, the U.S. remains

---

[35] Source:
http://www.bea.gov/industry/gpotables/gpo_action.cfm

as the largest manufacturing country in the world. This demonstrates the fallacy of believing that U.S. manufacturing has been in decline for many years, and is likely to die in the near future. What gave rise to such a fallacy? Over the years manufacturing employment has actually declined. That raises the immediate question of how manufacturing output could be growing while at the same time manufacturing employment was decreasing? The answer is that the productivity in the manufacturing industry was soaring, According to information from the National Association of Manufacturers over the past two decades manufacturing productivity has grown by 94%, considerably faster than the rest of the U.S. business sector, where productivity grew by 38% over the same period[36].

So what was seen was the drop in manufacturing employment. Politicians made a lot of fuss about that, and many of them falsely blamed it on outsourcing. To popular acclaim, there were campaigns to "buy American" and to stop "shipping American jobs overseas." But what was not seen was the growth in U.S. manufacturing output. Since it was not seen, it was simply assumed away without question. So once again we see a significant economic fallacy because of what is not seen.

3. Outsourcing Is Harmful

Many people are opposed to outsourcing, and believe that it is harmful to the American economy and the American worker. In late 2010 Ohio's

---

[36] Source:
http://www.industryweek.com/articles/the_face_of_american_manufacturing_14159.aspx

governor defended his order to ban offshoring of state government work, describing it as "common sense". The governor stated that "no one in India, or anywhere else, is going to tell the citizens of Ohio where we can create jobs or how we can spend our resources." How valid is this opposition to outsourcing? Imagine that a tailor takes ten hours to make a physician's navy blazer, and the physician could do the job in eight hours. The tailor earns $11 per hour, and the physician earns $300 per hour. Does it make sense for the physician to make the blazer, or to hire the tailor to make the blazer? The answer is clear: the physician can earn more money in just one hour ($300) than the tailor can make in 10 hours (10 x $11 = $110). So it definitely pays the physician to outsource the making of the blazer to the tailor. The physician has a comparative advantage in medical practice, and should therefore concentrate on practicing medicine. In fact, most of us practice our trade or profession, and outsource our purchases to other suppliers. For example, we buy our autos from auto dealers, our clothing from stores, and our computers from electronics outlets. Few of us make our own shoes or build our own furniture. Instead, we just do what we do best, and buy the rest. So common sense says we should outsource most of our needs rather than become self-sufficient.

Now imagine that our physician lives in the U.S. and our tailor lives in Hong Kong. Does that change the decision to outsource the blazer? No, it does not. The physician is still better off practicing medicine and buying the blazer from the tailor in Hong Kong. That seems to be common sense – unlike the "common sense" of the governor of Ohio. Where did the governor of Ohio go wrong? He focused upon what could be seen: namely the loss of Ohio government jobs to India. But he missed (or ignored) what could not be seen: the savings to Ohio taxpayers from outsourcing state tasks to India. No question that some Ohio government workers would lose their jobs. But – just like the physician in our example – the savings to the Ohio taxpayers would far outweigh the losses of the Ohio government workers. The logical solution would be to use a portion of those tax savings to retrain the Ohio government workers for other jobs. In that case, everyone is better off by virtue of the outsourcing: the Ohio taxpayers save money, the Ohio government workers get new and probably more secure jobs, and Indian workers get more business.

In short, outsourcing gets a bad rap when we focus only upon what is seen. But once we take into account what is unseen, then outsourcing looks very different. The gains from outsourcing will usually be more than sufficient to pay for the retraining of workers who are displaced and need new employment. We might add that economic research has shown that outsourcing is not the main destroyer of jobs. By far the greatest destroyer of jobs is new technology. Just ask the workers who used to be typists (before typewriters were replaced by computers) or telephone operators (before operator telephone exchanges were replaced by computers) or bookbinders (before e-books became prevalent). New technology is the main destroyer of jobs, which is plain to see. But perhaps unseen is that new technology is also the main creator of new jobs, which had not even been thought to exist. Just think of the workers busy making Apple iPads, 4g smart cell phones, and handy portable GPS units.

4. Energy Independence Is An Immediate Objective

The popular slogan "energy independence" sounds appealing and sensible. The U.S. imports over 60% of its oil from foreign suppliers, and much of foreign oil comes from politically hazardous and possibly hostile regimes. So energy independence has a definite political attractiveness. For example, President Obama stated that: "Washington may not be ready to get serious about energy independence, but I am. And so are you. And so are the American people." [37] But however desirable this goal may be, it is severely impractical and little more than an alluring fantasy. Energy independence is a collection of several fallacies. One fallacy is that ethanol is part of a solution to heavy dependence on foreign oil.

Federal government efforts to promote biofuel production have significantly increased output. Generously-subsidized ethanol producers now use so much corn that corn prices have skyrocketed, contributing to inflation here at home and food riots abroad. Despite the evident failings of transforming food into fuel, most politicians—and the American public by and large —still think "energy independence" is a goal we can and should, achieve. On first impression, the argument seems

---

[37] Source:
http://www.whitehouse.gov/blog_post/serious_about_energy_independence/

convincing. Imported oil, which is 60% of the oil we use, renders our economy vulnerable to dangers throughout the world. It also provides billions of dollars to anti-American countries like Iran, Russia, Saudi Arabia, and Venezuela.

But second thoughts reveal that energy independence is a wildly unrealistic goal. We have no satisfactory substitute for the imported oil we are dependent upon. The crash programs that claim to rapidly replace imported oil such as "clean coal," biofuels, and nuclear power, all have significant environmental and political dangers. Further, even if we had effective substitutes ready, it would require many years and great quantities of energy, including oil, to replace all the vehicles, pipelines, refineries, and other elements of the old oil infrastructure. None of this is new information.. But the mantra of "energy independence" offers political cover for a whole raft of dubious initiatives. Ethanol makers lobby for massive subsidies. Electric utilities and coal producers push for clean coal and a nuclear revival, although there is no safe solution for disposing of hazardous nuclear waste. Not only do electric utilities and nuclear interests lobby vigorously, but renewable energy producers like solar and wind power use suspicions of foreign oil to promote their own products, — even though many of these techniques are unreliable and far from being adequate replacements for imported oil.

If we devoted our entire corn crop to producing ethanol, the resulting ethanol fuel would replace less than a sixth of the gasoline we currently use.[38] Other potential fuels are even more marginal. Hydrogen was at one time considered a natural successor to oil. But hydrogen is complex to refine and handle. In fact, a study determined that a gallon of hydrogen contains nearly 25 percent less energy than was consumed producing it.

Ethanol is an easy target to discredit. But the fact is that all of the suggested alternatives are plagued by substantial environmental hazards or other external costs. Wind requires vast amounts of land; and kills flocks of birds which fly into the blades of windmills and get chopped into bits. In any case, wind is sporadic, electricity is difficult and expensive to store, and therefore wind power needs backup power support from dependable coal or nuclear power plants. Solar-cell manufacturing is chemically intensive, and sunshine too is very sporadic in nature, which – like wind power – requires backup power support from dependable coal or nuclear power plants. Nuclear energy is beset by safety and security concerns. Finally, the U.S. could fuel its entire car fleet with synthetic gasoline made from abundant coal. The technology for this certainly exists, but it is far from cost-effective, and synfuel gasoline-from-coal is even more ecologically hazardous than oil. The lesson is that energy independence seems feasible and attractive from what is seen. But what is unseen quickly disillusions us about this surface appeal. Once we dig below the surface, it becomes readily apparent that energy independence is a facile but

---

[38] Source: http://motherjones.com/print/15425

thoroughly impractical goal for many years to come. Maybe some geek in Silicon Valley will come up with a brilliant technological solution to energy independence. That is a wonderful dream. But it would be foolish to pin our hopes on such a dream.

5. Other Fallacies

There is no shortage of popular economic fallacies. We could cite many more fallacies, of which there is no shortage. For example "healthcare reform" is not about healthcare. Our health is largely in our own hands, and not in the hands of politicians or medical professionals. Rather, health depends upon good nutrition, sufficient exercise, and avoiding toxic substances like nicotine from smoking and not engaging in dangerous activities, such as racing automobiles or motorcycles. Further, "healthcare reform" is not about medical care, which is largely diagnosing illnesses and prescribing medications or performing surgery. Actually "healthcare reform" is about providing medical insurance for the uninsured.

Fallacies are often intentional efforts by politicians to mislead voters by using language that sounds good, but which is deceptive. Words that are frequently attached to political moves are "fair" (which sounds fine, but is meaningless because people have varying ideas about what is "fair") and "infrastructure" which implies fixing potholes in highways, replacing rusty rivets in bridges, and other repairs and maintenance of public facilities. But politicians do not gather votes or win elections by getting potholes fixed or rusty rivets replaced.

They much prefer new roads and new bridges to be built, whether or not actually needed. These new roads and new bridges can be named the Nancy Pelosi Highway or the Harry Reid Memorial Bridge. No-one names fixed potholes or replaced rivets after politicians. After all, new roads and new bridges can be seen. But fixed potholes or replaced rivets remain unseen.

Another loaded word is "greed." In the 2010 sequel to the movie "Wall Street" capitalist villain Gordon Gekko says: "Somebody reminded me I once said 'greed is good,'" Gordon tells a crowd of future business leaders. "Now, greed is legal." It is customary to accuse corporate executives of "greed" especially when they receive huge sums of money as compensation. The purpose here is not to defend the honor of corporate executives. Like all people, they include both the good and the bad. But it is appropriate to note that seldom are movie stars, rock stars or prominent professional athletes castigated for "greed" although they receive compensation as big – or even bigger – than that of corporate executives. Neither are politicians or government officials accused of "greed" even though some politicians have held political office for their entire careers, never held a private sector job, and have been found guilty of ethical and legal transgressions. The same free pass also seems to be given to government officials who have failed to pat their taxes or who have misused their obligations to serve the voters. The epithet of "greed" seems to be used as a weapon of class warfare directed against corporate executives, but not against movie stars, rock stars or prominent professional athletes. A likely reason is that the work product of movie stars, rock stars or prominent professional athletes is easily seen, but the work product of corporate executives is not seen. In that case, "greed" seems to be yet another economic fallacy based on focusing on what is seen, but missing what is unseen.

Chapter Summary

The main points of Chapter 4 are as follows:

People who would never venture to express an opinion on rocket science or brain surgery or nuclear physics have no hesitation in confidently making pronouncements on major, complex economic issues. They are often in error, but seldom in doubt. . The purpose of this chapter is to help people to avoid falling into error by understanding that:

1.   Economics is not subjective guesswork or personal opinion. It is based on logic, factual evidence, and careful analysis. Its principles are objective, verifiable, and able to survive any test or challenge. Economics is not superficial or cursory or trivial. It is developed only by meticulous research, thorough investigation and profound deliberation. Economics requires years of education, study, experience and dedication – just like becoming an expert in rocket science or brain surgery or nuclear physics.

Economics deals with what is seen, and what is not seen. Below are several popular economic fallacies. They are fallacies because they are based only upon what is seen. In order to see through these fallacies it is necessary to consider what is not seen. Examples of these fallacies are as follows:

1. Price controls are effective
2. U.S. Manufacturing is in decline
3. Outsourcing is harmful
4. Energy independence is an immediate objective.
5. Greed occurs in business, but not in show business, sports or politics.

The above statements are neat, plausible and wrong. All are fallacies aimed to dupe those gullible members of the public, who are satisfied to view just what is seen. Only when one carefully considers what is unseen does one gets the true picture. Watch out for words that may sound genuine, but .which are misleading, such as "fair" or "healthcare" or "infrastructure."

Chapter 5

Federal, State or Local Government?

We make a living by what we get, but we make a life by what we give. Winston Churchill

In earlier chapters we showed that government should provide only public goods that the private sector is unable to supply. But we have not yet dealt with the question of how the functions of government should be split between the federal, state and local governments of the U.S. One important characteristic of the federal government is that it an absolutely pure monopoly because there is one and only one federal government. Monopoly is always good for the monopolist, but not necessarily good for anyone else. Free of pressure from competitors, the monopolist has little incentive to be efficient or innovative. Monopoly means never to have to say sorry. In sharp contrast, vigorous competition keeps the pressure on competitors to be continually efficient and innovative.

In these circumstances, the functions of the monopolist federal government should be as few as possible and all possible government functions should be performed by the state or local governments. But that leaves the question of which functions should be carried out by state governments, and which functions should be carried out by local governments? As we have previously noted the federal government seems remote and unresponsive to the voters. This suggests that all possible government functions should be assigned to local governments, because local governments are closest to local voters, most familiar with local issues and local conditions, and should therefore be most responsive to local voters. Further, there is competition between adjacent local governments. If any local voter is disappointed with his or her local government, he or she can vote with their feet, and move to an adjacent area. This competition between local governments makes them more likely to be responsive to local voters.

Probably a little less competitive with their peers than local governments are state governments. But state governments are still competitive with one another, and if they are sufficiently disappointed state voters can vote with their feet and move to a different state if need be. That gives us a logical order in which government tasks should be assigned to governments. First, as many government tasks as possible should be performed by local governments. Second, government tasks that cannot be assigned to local governments should be assigned to state governments. Third, only government duties that cannot be performed by state governments should be assigned as a last resort to the federal government. By adhering to those priorities we make governments as competitive as possible.

Nullification

A further remedy against federal government taxation without representation is state nullification. State nullification is the concept that the states can and must prevent the enforcement of unconstitutional federal laws within their borders[39].Nullification is fully described in the book entitled "Nullification: How to Resist Federal Tyranny in the 21st Century" by Thomas E. Woods, Jr. (Published by: Regnery Press, June 28, 2010). The concept of nullification is far from new. Distinguished Americans including Thomas Jefferson used nullification in the Kentucky Resolutions of 1798 and 1799 to stop the federal government from

Says, among other distinguished Americans. His draft of the Kentucky Resolutions of 1798 first introduced the word "nullification" into American political life, and follow-up resolutions in 1799 employed Jefferson's formulation that "nullification…is the rightful remedy" when the federal government goes beyond its constitutional powers. In the Virginia Resolutions of 1798, James Madison said the states were "duty bound to resist" when the federal government violated the Constitution.

But even earlier supporters of the U.S. Constitution at the Virginia ratifying convention of 1788 assured Virginians that they would be "exonerated" if the federal government attempted to impose "any supplementary condition" upon them by exercising powers over and above the ones the states had delegated to it. Patrick Henry and later Jefferson both emphasized these safeguards that Virginians had been assured of at their ratifying convention.

---

[39] Source: http://www.thomasewoods.com/learn-about-state-nullification/

As Jefferson pointed out, if the federal government is permitted to hold a monopoly on deciding the limit of its own powers, it will never limit its powers. The federal government has a clear conflict of interest in judging the extent of its own powers. It will continue to grow – despite elections, the separation of powers, and other checks and balances designed to limit government power. In his well-known Report of 1800, James Madison reminded Virginians and fellow Americans that the judicial branch was not perfect, and that a remedy must be found in case all three branches of the federal government exceed their constitutional limits.

Almost half of all U.S. states nullified the REAL ID Act of 2005. A fourth of all U.S. states have effectively defied the federal government over medical marijuana. Nullification initiatives of all kinds, involving the recent health care legislation, cap and trade, and the Second Amendment are appearing everywhere.

It is imperative to stop the relentless expansion of Leviathan before it is too late..

Chapter Summary

The main points of Chapter 5 are as follows:

We developed a logical order in which government tasks should be assigned to governments.
1. First, as many government tasks as possible should be performed by local governments.
2. Second, government tasks that cannot be assigned to local governments should be assigned to state governments.

3. Third, only government duties that cannot be performed by state governments should be assigned as a last resort to the federal government.
4. By adhering to those priorities we make governments as competitive as possible.

Finally we explained nullification to stop the relentless expansion of Leviathan before it is too late.

Chapter 6

Summary and Conclusions

Government, even in its best state, is but a necessary evil; in its worst state, an intolerable one.
Thomas Paine

Summary of Chapter 1

1. Thomas Paine's book "Common Sense" was a significant part of the inspiration for the 1776 American Revolution. It protested against taxation by the British crown without representation in the British parliament.

2. Today we seem to have come full circle in being under an unresponsive federal government of reckless spenders who have dug our nation into a vast fiscal hole that foreshadow unsustainable future taxes that neither our children nor our grandchildren can afford to pay.

3. Rather than acting responsibly to cut federal expenditures, our irresponsible politicians are likely to ration healthcare by denying costly but necessary medical procedures, and by launching inflation by rashly printing excessive amounts of money.

4. This raises a number of questions, such as:
    a. Is there an optimal size of government for economic prosperity and growth?

b. If so, what size should government be in relation to the total economy?

c. Which functions in the economy are best performed by the government, and which functions should not be performed by government?

d. How should government functions be divided among federal, state, and local governments?

e. What fact-based evidence and logical arguments exist in order for us to best decide these important issues?

The purpose of this book is to try and answer these questions. We begin with Chapter 2, which discusses whether government or the private sector should be responsible for allocating scarce economic resources to the infinite demands of producers and consumers.

<u>Summary of Chapter 2</u>

1. In practice, virtually all economies are mixed, with some activities carried out by the government, and other activities carried out in the private sector. So the issue of government sector and private sector becomes which economic activities should be performed by government, and which economic activities should be performed in the private sector?

2. The countries that enjoy the most economic freedom from government intervention are the most economically prosperous. The countries that enjoy the

least economic freedom from government intervention are the least economically prosperous.

3. Private goods should be provided only by the private sector. And public goods must be provided by government because they cannot be provided by the private sector.

4. It has been shown that government has vital functions to perform in the economy by providing military defense and the rule of law. Why should government not go much further and provide many more goods? That would certainly be the view of socialism, communism and fascism. But there many good reasons to reject this view.

5. Reasons why government should provide only public goods include:
   a. The agency problem.
   b. The "skin in the game" issue.
   c. Private sector innovation versus public sector inertia.
   d. The tragedy of the commons problem.
   e. The drift towards crony capitalism.
   f. The urge to "do something!"
   g. The repeated failure of well-intended government programs.

6. Government interference in free enterprise does damage rather than good.

Summary of Chapter 3

This chapter examined some reasons why all economic activity possible should be pursued in the private sector, and not in the government sector. These reasons are as follows:

1. Wealth production. Economic transactions in the free enterprise private sector are wealth-producing for all parties, which is not necessarily the case in the government sector.
2. Skin in the game. In the private sector parties win or lose with their own money. They are prudent because they have skin in the game. In the government sector parties use other people's (the taxpayers') money. They are reckless because they have no skin in the game.
3. Unintended consequences. Many programs have the best of motives, but result in adverse unintended consequences. In the private sector, firms are rewarded for success and penalized for failure, which puts a premium on caution and good sense. In the government sector politicians are not held to account for unintended consequences of foolhardy policies. Since there are no penalties for failure, there is little incentive for politicians to exercise caution and good sense.
4. Centralized Decision Making. Communism, socialism and fascism all are rigidly dedicated to centralized decision-making by the few officials at the top. In sharp contrast, capitalism is characterized by decentralized decision-making by individuals regardless of whether they are at the top or the bottom or any other place. The few officials at the top are no match for the most innovative and

entrepreneurial individuals in an entire country. Therefore it is no surprise that every communist, socialist, and fascist economy has been a serious disaster. Until China and Russia dropped major components of their communist ideology, they were economic failures unable to feed, shelter or clothe their citizens.

5. Spontaneous Order Versus Rules and Plans. It is the price system that lets the free enterprise capitalist economy function spontaneously but with the precision of a Swiss watch – even though there is no watchmaker. There is only a self-organizing system that automatically creates spontaneous order. The free enterprise private sector self-organizing system is just like other self-organizing systems, such as the ocean tides, the seasons, the blood circulatory system, and a beehive. No government can possible outperform the spontaneous, self-organizing free enterprise market.

6. Monopoly Or Competition. When transactions are entered into in the competitive free enterprise private sector, they tend to be moral in nature. But when transactions are entered into in the government sector, they are under a monopoly. Unfortunately monopoly lacks the incentive for ethical behavior. That is another reason that all economic activity possible should be pursued in the private sector, and not in the government sector.

The reasons summarized above are why all economic activity possible should be pursued in the private sector. These are yet more reasons why economic activity is best performed in the private sector as far as possible, and why the government should not interfere with the economy, either by owning and operating the means of production, or attempting to regulate economic activity in the private sector. But it is not necessary to belabor the point any further because that would only be repetition – this solution has already been demonstrated many times over.

Summary of Chapter 4

1. People who would never venture to express an opinion on rocket science or brain surgery or nuclear physics have no hesitation in confidently making pronouncements on major, complex economic issues. They are often in error, but seldom in doubt. . The purpose of this chapter is to help people to avoid falling into error by understanding that:

2. Economics is not subjective guesswork or personal opinion. It is based on logic, factual evidence, and careful analysis. Its principles are objective, verifiable, and able to survive any test or challenge. Economics is not superficial or cursory or trivial. It is developed only by meticulous research, thorough investigation and profound deliberation. Economics requires years of education, study, experience and dedication – just like becoming an expert in rocket science or brain surgery or nuclear physics.

Economics deals with what is seen, and what is not seen. Below are several popular economic fallacies. They are fallacies because they are based only upon what is seen. In order to see through these fallacies it is necessary to consider what is not seen. Examples of these fallacies are as follows:

1. Price controls are effective
2. U.S. Manufacturing is in decline
3. Outsourcing is harmful
4. Energy independence is an immediate objective.

The above statements are neat, plausible and wrong. All are fallacies aimed to dupe those gullible members of the public, who are satisfied to view just what is seen. Only when one carefully considers what is unseen does one gets the true picture. Watch out for words that may sound genuine, but .which are misleading, such as "fair" or "healthcare" or "infrastructure."

<u>Summary of Chapter 5</u>

We developed a logical order in which government tasks should be assigned to governments.

1. First, as many government tasks as possible should be performed by local governments.
2. Second, government tasks that cannot be assigned to local governments should be assigned to state governments.
3. Third, only government duties that cannot be performed by state governments should be assigned as a last resort to the federal government.

4. By adhering to those priorities we make governments as competitive as possible.

Finally we explained nullification to stop the relentless expansion of Leviathan before it is too late.

The first American Revolution was caused by taxation without representation. We have come full circle – once more we have taxation without representation. Therefore the time has once more come for an American Revolution.

About the Author

Les Livingstone earned MBA and Ph.D. degrees at Stanford University. He is a CPA (licensed in NY and TX).

Les has been recognized as an expert on Finance, Economics & Accounting by numerous federal and local courts in a large number of U.S. states. These states include Arizona, California, Florida, Georgia, Massachusetts, New York, Pennsylvania, South Dakota & Texas, as well as Washington DC.

Since 1991 Les has directed his own consulting firm, specializing in Damage Estimation for large-scale Commercial Litigation and in Business Valuation. He has served as a Consulting or Testifying Expert in many cases, and has testified in Federal and State courts in Arizona, California, Florida, Georgia, Illinois, Massachusetts, New York, Rhode Island, and Texas. He has also testified before Federal government agencies including the FTC, FERC, as well as the Public Utilities Commission of Texas.

His previous experience in accounting, finance and business includes the following:

- Babson College: Professor of Accounting and Chairman, Division of Accounting & Law.
- The MAC Group (now Cap Gemini/Ernst & Young Consulting), an international management consulting firm specializing in design and implementation of business strategy for major corporations: Principal.

- Coopers & Lybrand (now PricewaterhouseCoopers), Partner.
- Georgia Institute of Technology: Fuller E. Callaway Professor of Accounting.
- Ohio State University: Arthur Young Distinguished Professor of Accounting.

Publications:

Author or coauthor of:

- About 50 articles in leading professional journals.
- Numerous chapters in authoritative handbooks.
- 18 books.
- Recent books include:
- *The Economics of Public Choice, 2010,*
- *Ethical Decision Making*, 2009,
- *Finance Made Easy*, 2009 and
- *The Economics of Energy*, 2008

  All published by and available from Lulu.com http://www.lulu.com/ and also from Amazon.com

- *Economics Made Easy*, 2007 and
- *Guide to Business Valuation*, 2007

  Both published by Freeload Press and available from http://www.textbookmedia.com/Default.asp x and also from Amazon.com

- *The Portable MBA in Finance and Accounting*

  A selection of the Book of the Month Club, the Fortune Book Club and the Money Book Club. The paperback edition was a selection of the Quality Paperback Book Club.

  The 4th edition was published in 2009 by John Wiley & Sons, Inc., Hoboken, NJ. This book has been translated into Mandarin and Cantonese Chinese, Indonesian, Japanese, Portuguese, Russian, and Spanish.